I0559320

Leaving the Clouds

LEAVING
THE
CLOUDS

A book of poetry by
TARA OSH

Leaving the Clouds: A Book of Poetry © 2024
Tara OSH. All rights reserved.

These poems are the intellectual property of the
author. Unauthorized reproduction, distribution,
or use of this poem without the author's explicit
written consent is prohibited.

For permissions, contact
theoshwriter@gmail.com.

Publication Date: July 2024

Paperback ISBN: 978-1-955541-54-1
eBook ISBN: 978-1-955541-55-8
Hardcover ISBN: 978-1-955541-56-5
LCCN: Pending

Published by FuzionPress
1250 E 115th Street
Burnsville, MN 55337
FuzionPress.com
612-781-2815

TABLE OF CONTENTS

Nature | 7

Life | 19

Contemplations | 33

Tormented Love | 57

Loving | 85

Love Past | 95

NATURE

Nature is not my natural place.
When others talk about their love of it, I smile listening while internally screaming about the absurdity of those claims of a beautiful pond, which is the breeding ground for blood-sucking mosquitos. Only vampires Can appreciate the taste of my life source. No thank you, I'd like to keep it in my own veins, please.

Nature is not my natural place.
When others ooh and ah over the beautiful flowers saying "Come smell this amazing Jasmine." Instead, I hold my tongue from revealing that when the flower starts to die, it smells the same as dead semen and I have yet to find anyone who likes that smell if they are being really honest with themselves.

Nature is not my natural place.
When one says how much they love the look of that or this tree, a leaf, or a petal, I somehow feel the need to warn them that the bark may scratch, it could be poisonous, or it will eventually fall onto the ground and no longer be. In fact, touch at your own risk, just like with me.

Nature is not my natural place.
Listen to the birds or the whispers of the trees. My reply is what's wrong with silence? People are already noisy enough, why do I need to also take in the sounds of other living beings?

Nature is not my natural place.

But, of all the senses, sight is the one I could not live without. I can see the peace of the water feature and taste the cooling water on a warm day. I can visualize a pleasing aroma of the newly blooming flower. I can imagine the texture of the rock wall and falling ivy. I can envision the words whispered between the trees and the birds in the sky.

So, you see my head is already full of all these senses and I have barely left my seat!

I am not a lover of nature
because I'm allergic
to all its feature.

Yet,
I can hear the trees
whisper stories in their rhetoric
of the past, present to the birds and bees.

When the seasons change,
I feel the warmth of summer sun
cool breezes of fall and spring, and the winter temperature
range.

To the flowers that bloom
I bask in their various colors
and rejoice in the goodbye of grey gloom.

As the birds fly through the air
with morning songs and little hops
I cannot help but stare.

Still, I'm really not a lover of nature,
but perhaps I shall admit
that I give thanks to the ironic Creator.

Oh the sniffing, the sneezing!
Thankfully, I'm not yet wheezing.

It's that time of year
when being outside causes fear.

How long can I last
before the final pollen is cast?

I try to stay upbeat
never wanting to admit defeat.

But, alas, I cannot keep up the fight
as my puffy eyes decrease my sight.

I cannot pretend anymore it is funny
that my nose is always runny.

So, it's back inside I go
losing again to nature – my greatest foe!

Rain falls outside the window
  As I look out over the green meadow

Over hills and treetops
  At the grey sky and olive crops

The return from a long trip
  Is always filled with a reality grip

Time to do the daily chores
  All those things that bores

The mind, the body which is whining
  That in 24 hours it is not striving

To get up and get things done
  While wishing I could just see the sun.

It's grey today
and the wind blows
as I sit watching the trees sway
a sense of gloom threatens and grows.

Days like this are likely necessary,
but it is hard to still be merry.

On the bright side,
here I am nice and warm
letting the pen be my guide
as these words form.

When we are above the clouds
The sun shines and the sea of white
Rolls to eternity
The soft pillows of fluff lay the ground
For the angels to roam and play
It is a small piece of heaven that
We can touch

In a plane
In our dreams

Inevitably we must descend
The puffs stretch into wisps
Then turbulence hits
As our view becomes blocked

We are blinded into a fog
No end can be seen
We can only bounce around
Bumping along waiting for the eventual clearing

Then we pass through
Our fears of the unknown no longer legitimate
For we continue to fly

Soaring toward our destination with relief
With excitement

The clouds that were just below
Are now above
Their cover is a promise
As the angels look down
Like a blanket and lid of protection

We continue on
Leaving the clouds for
Another day

Outside is grey and gloom,
        much like my mood.
There's no reason why
        yet I feel like I could cry.

Sometimes too much chatter
        can alter the course of the matter
So that what could have been happy
        somehow becomes crappy.

Now I hide in my room
        avoiding any pending doom
As the shadows pass by
        until I can smile with a sigh.

The sky is a perfect blue
As I make my way back to you.

The clouds make a perfect blanket of white
As I imagine being in your arms tonight.

The sun shines brightly through the window
As I accept what my heart already did know –

No matter how scared I might feel
These feelings we have are for real.

A walk in the sun
To get a breath of fresh air
Is how it was begun.

Connected as friends
Laugh and hang out together
Nosotros hablamos en español también!

Smiles, hugs and little chats
Made me feel comfortable to share
More than just my fear of ending up with just cats.

I have no expectations;
Desire no pressure or dramas,
Just feel good without any hesitation.

So, I continue to walk in the sunshine
Enjoying the warmth and ease of
Being with you, holding your hand in mine.

LIFE

They look
They stare
They smile
They hiss
They laugh
They propose
They walk with an air of importance

Am I just an object to them?
Am I just a vessel for pleasure to them?
Am I meant to be submissive to them?
Am I valued at all as a human being to them?

Some say it is culture.
Some say it is religion.
Some say it is the color of my skin.
Some say it is the slant of my eyes.
Some say it is just the way it is.

Am I to just ignore it?
Am I to just accept it?
Am I to condone it?
Am I to devalue my own humanity for it?

Insh'Allah, in God I trust, in Jesus' name
I pray

For I am not just an object.
For I am not just a vessel of pleasure.
For I am not willing to be submissive due to my gender.
For I am a woman

Who values herself
Who celebrates her beauty
Who respects herself as a human being.

Everything has a purpose
Time is never wasted
For loving is a gift

Everything has a purpose
People may come and go
But friendships are a gift

Everything has a purpose
Words are not lost
In conversations we find a gift

Everything has a purpose
A gentle touch is never unwanted
Kindness is a gift

When we love
When we are friends
When we speak with others
When we touch one another

It is a gift
Everything has a purpose

The words echo throughout the town
En masse the people stop to pray

Where has the voice gone? From whence does it come?

Do they all believe in the call?
Will these boys become men if the time came for them to
stand for honor, country and Islam?

Amidst the words, the voices, the prayers
Where am I?
Where do I stand? Where is my Father, Lord of all?

The horns honk
The sirens blare
And I do not care.

The men gawk
The people stare
And I do not care.

The temperatures can conk
The weather may always be fair
But still I do not care.

For nothing can knock
Me out of this state, so rare
Because it's for you

That I care.

Another day
A new cafe

Somewhere to sit
And, be quiet for a bit

Movement is constant
Noises do not relent

Yet it's a chosen space
As an occasional happy place

To watch the world go by
Trying not to ask why

That person does this
Or, what they might wish

Instead, just observing
And learning

About the intricacies of life
Whether with or without strife

We, humans, carry on
I do wonder, though, for how long

Life just is – a wandering of this world
　　　　trying to discover what will unfurl.

Life just is – a string of experiences
　　　　some good, some bad, some open doors, others
fences.

Life just is – a chance to learn
　　　　about ourselves, about others, about on what we
should concern.

Life just is – but a brief moment
　　　　and of what is beyond us, we only have a hint.

Life just is – the here, the now
　　　　and each day, I simply try to survive it somehow.

Another cafe
　　　　Another day

Of wandering
　　　　Of writing

Claiming some time
　　　　Claiming this rhyme

As I observe the rhythm
　　　　As I watch all of them

The people here in Wimbledon
　　　　The life of the United Kingdom

There's a thrill in the charts
          The ups and downs of the lines

There's a thrill in the stars
          The twinkling lights blow our minds

Whether by nature or man
          We are impressed with all kinds.

Some used to think it was a sign from the gods
        When the sun and moon aligned

Some used to make sacrifices to ward off evil
        When the sun and moon aligned

Some used to believe the end was near
        When the sun and moon aligned

Now, we travel far and wide
        To see the sun and moon align

Now, we use technology to enhance the view
        To see the sun and moon align

Now, we dramatize and romanticize
What once was mystified
Looking through a protective lens with our eyes
Some blase while others are stupified

A sign to ward off an enhanced dramatic, romantic, mysterious
view of a colorized moment.

If only we saw the parallels … of our present universe.

What is it about the beach life
Seemingly free from any strife
Perhaps much like me these days as a housewife
Although you would rarely find me in the kitchen with a knife.

It's the laid back vibe
Where it's easy to scribe
Escaping all the daily gibe
With freedom to find your tribe

Or maybe it's the aspect of nature
Being close to something greater
Than ourselves - the grand creator
Feeling grateful for the Universe's labor

Whatever it is, I feel at home
Less restless or wanting to roam
A sense of calm is found with the sea foam
Giving space as we sit in ohm

I have a sensation
That some will call just my imagination
But I am closer to my end
Which for me does not offend

In a way I welcome the reprieve
As I've not got great things left to achieve
My life has been full
And there are no regrets to cull

CONTEMPLATIONS

Enjoy today,
        for life is short,
The elders say to the youth

Don't worry about today,
        for there's always tomorrow,
The optimists say to the pessimists.

The early bird
        gets the worm,
Says the early riser to the night owl.

We live in a time and space
        of contrast.
Overlooking the concept of balance.

So much effort vying for control.
        Up and down goes the see-saw, but too high or too
low
Nobody wins, everyone is going against the flow.

Those who sit in quiet, trying to
        Send out positive energy
Are also guilty of escapism in equal measure.

Push, pull goes the
        tug of power

Make peace, not war, stop to smell a flower.

Understand what this life
        is for

Yet, we seem to desire
        The constant angst
        The crying, gnashing of teeth,

When we could hug, laugh
        And lift each other up beneath

With a cover of love.

The past is gone
there is only today
and thoughts of tomorrow.

Yet the past still haunts us
affecting our decisions today
prohibiting us from the freedom of tomorrow.

Each time there is something new
we think about the past
forget to live for today
and worry about tomorrow.

It is time to let go of the past
focus on the beauty of today
and hope for all the joys that may come tomorrow.

Some words are meant to bring laughter
Some words are meant to bring tears
Some words are meant to heal
Some words are meant to hurt
Some words…

are

lacking in expressing enough
lacking in accuracy of the feelings to be shared
lacking in hope
lacking in encouragement
lacking in ….

love

Words can be weapons
Words can be bridges
Words can be painful
Words can be uplifting
Words can be …

more than we will ever know or truly understand.

Today –
    Maybe I'll
    Study, work, play,
    Laugh, cry, smile,
    Go, stay.
    Worthwhile.
Heart –
    aches inside,
    wanting to start,
    feelings to confide,
    hating apart.
    Cried?
Mind –
    cannot drop
    countless thoughts entwined
    ready to pop
    concepts undefined.
    Stop?
Tomorrow's –
    another chance
    when time borrows
    opportunity for romance,
    denies sorrows
    Advance.

Passion and comfort
Excitement and stability
Spontaneity and consistency
Newness and trust

Balances to be made and found
Bringing my ideals to the ground
Of reality

Is it too much to want it all?
Is it too much to refuse to fall
Victim to hope's demise?
Surely there must be a compromise….

No time to think –

No time to sleep –

No time to dream –

No time to run –

No time to plan –

No time to eat –

No time to chat –

No time to be at peace –

No time….

and yet when we die we will have all the time in the world!

From the outside,
It shines like a new coin.

From the outside,
It runs like a well-oiled machine.

From the outside,
Everyone smiles.

From the outside,
Everyone is your friend.

Unfortunately, the inside is never
Quite what it seems,

From the outside.

He is the reason
       For the season

He has risen
       Indeed, he has risen

Happy Easter
       To the chocolate bunny feaster

Buona Pasqua
       A vino dalle acqua

There is no harm in believing
       Those things that need help conceiving

So what if it isn't true
       Makes no difference to me or you

The harm is in not allowing
       To whomever I may be bowing

Who are you or I to say
       What comes after our last day

So whether it is Jesus, God, Buddha or Allah
       In one spirit, we are united forevah

Go outside,
        the sun is shining!
Go outside,
        it's a beautiful day!
Go outside,
        the fresh air is good for you!

Says the extroverts,
        Says the outdoorsies,
                Says the annoying ones.

Stay inside,
        there's a book to read!
Stay inside,
        a story is bleeding onto the page!
Stay inside,
        it's calm, quiet, comforting!

Says the introverts,
        Says the indoorsies,
                Says the peaceful ones.

Choose for you.
Leave the others to it.
Go or stay, whichever is your way!

The writer longs for description
The painter craves expression
The sculptor aches for formation
The actor dreams of recognition

and to what end?

For whom do we describe our thoughts and feelings?
From whom do we need to be recognized?
For what do we desire to make form?
For what do we gain recognition?

is it to make the world better?
is it to leave our mark?

Is it possible for our creative angst to be relieved?

Here, there
	I am

Past, present, future
	I am

Everywhere and nowhere
	I am

I am
	soaring above in the clouds
	swimming in the waters below
	wafting in the gentle breeze
	blowing through the mighty trees

Whether here or over there
	I simply am.
In a version of myself in times forgotten or yet unknown
	here I am.
Within all spaces and in the voids
	still I am.

This is just who and where
	I am.

A year ago
     I was starting an adventure
A year ago
     I was buzzing with the unknown
A year ago
     I was longing for what I was leaving behind

Then, the year passed
     in a blur
The year passed
     with great perplexion
The year passed
     with the future always unsure

Now, somehow
     the world is spinning a little slower
Somehow
     life here is a little less annoying
Somehow
     my reasons for being here are a little clearer

To get here
>	I had to hurt
To get here
>	I had to hurt others
To get here
>	I had to endure
To get here
>	I had to be endured

But, at last
I'm here.
I'm happy.
I'm content.
I'm free.
I'm me.

I am alone
For the first time in my life
Before, I was a child
Then I became a wife

Now, I am alone
Living in a new place
Where there is only me
And no one knows my face

Sometimes I feel very alone
Wondering if I've made a mistake,
Am I out of my mind?
Is my future really mine to make?

Yet, I find in being alone
I am finding the real me
I am learning about who I am
I am finally feeling free

There are emotions that sit
     in waiting, revealing bit by bit

Expectations breed negativity
     but patience brings positivity

Like the spring buds of flowers
     all will be revealed in the right hours

Being aware
     avoids potential scares

That suddenly an emotion will show
     in a way we do not know

But all will be well
     you'll see - time will tell.

The gift of me-time can't be beat
      Time to the self, time to breathe
Chores can be done, like changing the sheets
      Or even just a pause to brush the teeth.

As an introvert, I cherish the silence
      A moment to escape the noisy violence
Of chatter, of competing energies
      Instead, enjoying the quiet synergies

With peace, a pause for all things
      To cease, to just being.

What happened to my dreams,
Where I used to imagine were in the clouds?

What happened to my faith,
Where I used to see His face in the clouds?

What happened to my voice,
Where I used to speak and sing to the clouds?

What happened to the joy,
Where I used to find in the clouds?

Today I am glad.
Today I am sad.
Today I am cheery.
Today I am teary.
Today I am smiling.
Today I am frowning.
Today I am happy.
Today I am sappy.

Today I have ups and downs
Tomorrow there will be no frowns!

The age-old question arises again
Can men and women really be friends?
Almost all of my friends are men
Does it mean there is always something there in the end?

I have new people in my life
Some are female, most are male
Yet, I already get the question to cause me strife
"What's going on with you two?" comes up without fail.

Yes, I hate to be single and alone
Yes, I would like to be in a relationship
Yes, I'd love to have someone to call my own
But, still I cherish even the simplest of friendships.

So, now I feel a bit of tension
There are men I am content to just hang with
There are men I'd like to give me more attention
Overall, I truly wonder if pure male/female relations is just a myth.

One year later
I still feel the ache
Like the shadows that haunt a grieving heart
Once something is broken
It's never really the same again

One year later
There is stiffness
From lack of use like sorrow
That wallows in a pool of darkness
It is easy to let the grooves deepen

One year later
The mind might forget
But the body remembers
And the soul is imprinted forever

There are triggers
There are passing moments
There are lingering clouds

Even one year later.

The threads that connect us
can vary from the thick to thin, thus
depending on the experience shared
that defines how much we've cared.

The presence of family brings the past
        Into the present, making it last.

Lingering in the memories
        Replaying the vents like a series.

Despite our attempts not to repeat
        Our histories, it can't be beat

When family knows us intimately
        Growing the roots that run deeply

Sometimes the hold is too tight
        Other times, it feels just right.

For that's the gift of family love
        It's the bonds that we are made of

Life experiences together
        That are like no other.

TORMENTED LOVE

A soft whisper
A gentle touch
A sweet caress
        Is all that I desire.

A pleasant conversation
A sharing of hearts
A feeling of trust
        Is all that I need.

A step closer
A heartbeat away
A sigh of contentment
        Is all that I hope.

I desire a subtle sweetness that encaptures passion.
I need both a best friend and a lover to trust.
I hope for open arms to complete the circle of love.

In all my life,
I've wanted to be
as I am with you

– Just me.

In all my life,
I've wanted to share
as I do with you

– Just me.

In all my life,
I've wanted to love
as I'm loved by you

as just me.

Sometimes I worry and fret
Sometimes I imagine what hasn't happened yet.

My heart still shudders at the memory
Of when you were away from me.

And there are times when the fear sets in
Will he still love me tomorrow…? But, then

I see you and you smile
Then I know all my worrying was not really worthwhile.

I try to understand
I try to empathize
I try to rationalize

Yet, my words get twisted
Yet, my voice gets lost
Yet, my heart gets pain

How can it be –
This change?
This stranger?
This feeling of loss?

The more I try, the less I sleep
The more I think, the less I understand
The more I rationalize, the less it makes sense

My love is the same
My passion is the same
My feeling is the same

So, why does it all feel different?

If you are always right
And I am always wrong,
Then why do we fight?

With all your tendencies
Towards arrogance, hypocrisy and idiocy,
Why won't you just see?

Perhaps, just possibly,
You might be wrong –
But, no, how could that be?

Getting to know you has been beyond words
You're more than I wished for
How you make me feel seems almost absurd.

As my breath catches at your touch
As my heart flutters at your smile
Making my mind stop from thinking too much.

So little time has passed since we first went out
Yet through our friendship I feel
I sort know what you're about.

What the future holds, I don't know
But I look forward to what may come
And I will go with the flow.

As the flutter continues in my heart
And the catch continues in my breath
I feel myself never wanting to be apart.

Have I told you too much?
Have I asked too much?
Have I expected too much?

My mind spins in circles
Wondering if I've ruined all that is good
Causing you to run away...

How do I stop myself from thinking?
How do I stop myself from worrying?
How do I stop myself from hurting?

My heart beats rapidly
Thinking of you and how you might be feeling
Hoping you'll not run away...

You said you would be willing to try
When it comes time to say good-bye.

You said you wouldn't share,
Does it mean that you really care?

You've told me of your family
And I find myself listening to you happily.

You allow for quiet moments to linger
Providing me with peace as I fidget with a finger.

You hold me close without a word
So that in just a short time, a night without you seems absurd.

My wall has not yet gone up, is it true?
My heart has not yet closed up, is it true?
My fear has not yet built up, is it true?

Is this really you?

The other night I laid and stared at your face
The other night I sighed a deep sigh in your embrace
The other night I found myself wanting to define
      Whether or not I am yours and you are mine.

Before this began, I was content to be alone
Before this began, I was happy for friendship to be the tone
Before this began, I was satisfied
      Or so I thought, or so I tried.

Now, I think of you all day
Now, I want you in every way
Now, I feel myself getting shy
      Wondering if you will know why.

Can I tell you all that's in my heart?
Can we last when we're apart?
Can I truly let you in?
      Is it safe to let this begin?

Almost a year ago a drunken statement made
Put into motion the uniting of our hearts.
Though time would pass and plans waylaid
To keep us physically apart,

Nothing could stop the emotions from colliding.
Nothing could stop the tears from falling.
Nothing could stop the aching.
Nothing can stop the loving.

Now we move forward at a rapid pace
Hoping for a future with each other
Planning how to always be face to face
And knowing somehow we'll find a way to be together.

Each day passes taking me further away
Yet a part of me wants to stay
Close by just to see
What might be.

A look in the eye
Brings a smile and a sigh
For it's quite a treat
To feel something so sweet.

What is this feeling?
Is it too soon to be dreaming?
How will I know if this is right?
Will it be worth a fight?

When I go
Will we know
If we want this to last,
Or is the time just too fast?

My heart is on hold
as each day passes
Waiting…

My mind races
as each day passes
Waiting…

Will my feelings turn cold?
Will loneliness be what I have to face?
For these answers, I am waiting…

"Take your time", I say,
But waiting is making me, crayzay!

Fear of hurt, failure, disappointment, sadness
Fear of the unknown
Fear of what might be or rather what might not be…

Fear

is what holds you back

from love

Despite the strong feelings
Despite the physical attraction
Despite the spiritual connection

Despite

these things you hold back

from love

How can you let it all go to waste?
How can you let it all pass us both by?
Why won't you even give it a try?
Why won't you even give it a chance?

How... Why...

can you hold back

from love?

For a moment I'd like to know you.
For a moment I'd like to meet you.
For a moment I'd like to be accepted by you.

For a moment I'd like to feel your arms.
For a moment I'd like to hear "I've missed you".
For a moment I'd like to be truly loved by you.

Will that moment ever come?

For a moment I'd like to know where I came from.
For a moment I'd like to feel as if I truly fit in.
For a moment I'd like to just be me.

But will that moment ever really come?

My heart is still paused in a hope.
But I fear with the negative is what I will have to cope.

"Don't overthink", I am told.
But I feel as if what was started could be turning cold.

Time is quickly passing by…
Tonight I let myself truly cry.

Too much I already care
Wanting to trust, to love is this snare.

Do you feel the same?
Or is it still too much to give this a name?

Soon a decision will have to be made
By then will what had begun start to fade?

The rain poured down
Like the tears on my face
I felt as if I was going to drown
As the taxi pulled away from your place

Still my heart is breaking
As I long for your arms
Every bone is aching
To feel your sweet calm

Everything is new
I should be excited about it
Yet all I can think of is you
Wondering if I can make here fit

If I knew that you are truly mine
I could endure this separation
And try to enjoy the time
Waiting, until our next meeting, with anticipation

Instead, I wonder if you will find
Someone else soon
Who will take your heart and mind
Away…

There is so much I want to say to you
And yet, I find it is not yet something I can do.

There is so much I want to feel
And yet, I find there are still pieces needing to heal.

There is so much I want to know
And yet, I am not certain where to go.

There is so much…and yet not enough.

It's all too much to bear
That each time I start to really care
My heart is rejected and broken
Memories are my only token

I've questioned if God just hates me
I've questioned if there is something I can't see
I've questioned if it's not me, then who?
'Cuz obviously, it's not just you.

All I want is to be loved and allowed to love
Of all things – time, space, location – for it to be above
Because I should be more than worth it
For me all things would be forfeit

Perhaps I ask too much
But must I wait for a never-to-come someday for such?
Is hope, faith and love really wrong?
Without these, I see no point to going on…

My heart still aches for him
Yet, my hope has begun to dim.

My heart is hesitant to move on
But maybe what we had is gone.

Am I aching for the unattainable?
Am I hesitating for something unbelievable?

There are no more words for me to say
Only the hole in my heart and tears stay…

The days are passing slowly
As I wonder how it will be

to see you
to touch you
to hold you
to just be with you

My heart feels torn
As I wonder what the future holds

should I stay
should I go
will you stay
will you come

It seems endless as I consider
Three months are left

to wonder
to ponder
to weigh
to convey

All that I feel.

Every day brings me closer
        to seeing you.
Every day brings me closer
        to touching you.

Every day takes me further
        from knowing what to do
Every day takes me further
        from deciding about you

Should we be in the same place?
Should we be daily face-to-face?
Should we be thinking about the future?
Should we be letting this relationship fully mature?

Some days I feel we are on the same page
Some days I feel you are hard to fully gauge
Some days I don't know how to be apart
Some days I don't know how to express all that is in my heart

Every day brings me closer
Every day takes me further
Should we always be together?
Some days I don't know how I feel.

There was a time when I didn't need to know
There was a time when I thought the answer was clear
There was a time when I imagined it didn't really matter
If I ever found you

There was a time when I didn't want to know
There was a time when I thought there were no answers to fear
There was a time when I imagined it would only make me sadder
If I ever found you

Now is a time when I know
Now is a time when I think you could've been near
Now is a time when I imagine and my dreams are shattered
Because I found you

I haven't seen your face
I haven't heard your voice
I haven't learned of the place
I haven't yet had the choice
To find you…

Upclose
In person
So far
And yet… so close

The time is coming when I will
Find you
And find me within you
Find me.

Oh how the tears wet my pillow
As my arms ache in the absence
That makes my heart droop like a weeping willow

As the sun sets each night
I dread the darkness rolling in
Knowing its the shadows I have to fight

Every part of me misses your presence,
Your eyes, your smile, your smell, your touch
Your breath, your laugh, your very essence

I try to stay active and busy
I try to plan things to do
I try and try that I go dizzy

But despite all my cries
All I can do
Is wait for the sun to rise

What is this feeling?
What is this fear?
What is this I both desire and dread?

My heart remembers the pain
My heart still feels the wounds
My heart longs for love

I ache for tenderness
I ache for a soft whisper
I ache to trust

My spirit cries out
My spirit longs
My spirit no longer wants to go alone

Who can my heart beat for?
Who can stop the aching?
Who can protect my spirit?

Are you willing to take my heart and not break it?
Are you willing to hold me close and never let go?
Are you willing to love me body and soul?

Is this for real?
A man who opens doors
A man who requests that I go first?

Is this for real?
A man who tells me his thoughts
A man who shares his feelings?

Is this for real?
A man who is very masculine, but
A man who appreciates style, quality and sense?

Is he for real?

LOVING

Loving you
    Is an easy and natural thing to do.

It's as if you are a part of me
    And into my soul you see.

I remember the day we met,
    You were intriguing and yet,

My thoughts were only on friendship
    Someone to share the beach with for a dip.

Anything more, I didn't think
    Was in the cards – until that drink….

My world changed forever.
    Then, when our ties seemed to sever –

Everything stopped.

I couldn't breathe.
I couldn't eat.
I couldn't sleep.

What was life without you?

At last, things feel as they should be
        Just you and me.
At last, there is calm and peace
        This feeling I hope will never cease.

There is a smile on my face
Put there by you

There is joy in my heart
Placed there by you

There are not adequate words to express
My feelings for you

How my heart aches to be
Next to you

How my body aches to be
Close to you

How my eyes ache to be
Gazing at you

It's as if…

…I've been waiting all my life for you.
…I've always known you deep within.
…I've never really known love before.

It's as if…

…you read my thoughts before I say them.
…you know my heart without the words.
…you have always loved me –

and I you.

They say laughter makes a
 healthy heart.

For me, being with you is
 just the start.

Not only do you make me
 laugh,

But you really are like
 my other half.

Where I am lacking
 You are abundant
Where I am weak
 You are strong

Time spent with you is
 never dull.

You make every part
 of me full.

I love you –
     both parts and whole.

All this to say –
     You are good for my soul.

You are my north star
as the Earth spins

You are my sun
as the clouds roll in

You are my pillar
as the ground moves and shifts

You are my direction
as the wind blows.

It's in your
embrace I feel safe

It's in your
hands I feel sure

It's in your
eyes I see security.

For you remain my constant
as life races on.

Deep in my gut is where I feel it
Deep in my soul is where I know it
Deep in my heart is where I keep it

This feeling
This connection
This love

When I'm with you
The world slows down

When I'm with you
The air feels lighter

When I'm with you
The darkness fades away

Into the laughter
Into the joy
Into the peacefulness

Of this feeling
Of this connection
Of this love

LOVE PAST

Caught in a whirlwind
You aroused feelings I never imagined
Could be
Inside me –

raw anger
deep hate
strong loathing
only disdain

for you

Once you were my only one
I never thought these emotions could come
Was it so hard to see –

my love
my devotion
my pain
my suffering

for you

Now you can only point a finger
Now only in the photos does our memory linger
Of what once was and will never again be.

You don't deserve this poem,
But because we once shared a home
Because we once shared a heart
I need to express our coming apart.

For years I denied the truth
For years I tried to be your Ruth
For years I hid the pain
For years I accepted I would never again feel the same.

Slowly my identity faded
Slowly my attitude became jaded
Slowly my confidence dwindled
Slowly my love for you could not be kindled.

The more you said you tried
The more I cried
The more you said you would get better
The more I felt my heart become deader

With every look at an unknown her
With every comment for me to dress sexier
With every night I slept alone
With every eye that would roam

I died, piece by piece inside
From everyone I chose the pain to hide
Because I wanted to respect you
Because I thought it was the right thing a wife should do

Now, I wonder what it was all for
Now, I'm glad we're not together anymore
Now, though I would probably still do it all again
Now, I know it's the best thing that it came to an end

It was when we moved to the City

That it began – the leaving of my heart from yours

It was when I found my own course
That it seemed away from you I ran without pity
It was when I started succeeding
That you began to lose your way
It was when "I love you" became harder to say
That for a separation was my pleading
It was when your stress was so high
That you looked at them, those two-dimensional women
It was when you would ask me to dress more feminine
That every piece of my heart and soul would cry
It was when I realized the laughter between us had died
That there was nothing to be saved
It was when our attempts to "fix" it became depraved
That I learned we both to each other had lied
It was when the lies became too much
That I knew it was time to give up
It was when there was nothing left to take from our cup
That I could no longer bear your touch
It was when our simple conversations turned into arguments
That the yelling and slamming was only the tip of my anger

It was when we both began at each other to point a finger
That it was time to end the torments
It was when I cheated on you
That you felt the intensity
It was when all was lost in our beauty
That you finally knew
We were not meant to be…

You've gone and I feel relief
Our time together was very brief
But filled with ups and downs
Sometimes I felt like I was going to drown

> in your kisses
> in our arguments
> in your eyes
> in our differences
> in your arms
> in our opposites

You said you really care about me
But how can that be?
I asked you, "What does that mean?"
For this was never what it may seem….

> did we ever date?
> did we ever have a relationship?
> did you ever understand my heart wasn't yours?
> did you ever accept we could never really be?

You are gone now
I hope that somehow
All the pieces will mend
As we stay friends.

Eight years have past
Many of our family and friends gathered
Not knowing our lives were haphazard
Yet, we have made it last.

Our love is strong
Our friendship is the best
Life with you is full of zest
Marrying you was far from wrong.

To many more happy years
Filled with adventure
And excitement into the future
A kiss, a toast with these joyful tears.

It wasn't until the end was near
That it became so clear
Our hearts are intertwined
So strong is the connection of our minds

A friend, a lover, a confidante
A laugh, a kiss, a shoulder to cry on
All these moments we share
All these emotions seemed to come from nowhere

Yet as we weave our way
It feels only natural each day
To allow ourselves to do
Whatever it takes to say "I love you"